A First-Start® Easy Reader

This easy reader contains only 58 different words, repeated often to help the young reader develop word recognition and interest in reading.

a	dream	liked	them
all	fell	love	this
and	for	now	to
animals	go	old	tree
apple	good	people	trees
apples	grew	plant	under
Appleseed	grow	planted	up
are	he	see	walked
around	helped	seeds	want
asleep	him	slept	way
boy	I	stars	what
called	in	story	who
children	into	that	will
clothes	is	the	wore
down	Johnny		

Johnny Appleseed

by Tamar Mays

illustrated by Dana Regan

Troll

"Who planted this apple tree?"

5

"This tree is old. This is the story. A boy called Johnny fell asleep . . ."

Johnny fell asleep under a tree.
"What a good dream!"

"In the dream I see apple trees.
I see apple trees all around."

"Children love apples.

Animals love apples.
I want to plant apple trees all around."

"I want apples for all the children.

I want apples for all the animals."

"I will plant apple seeds.

The seeds will grow into apple trees."

"I will go up and down.

I will go this way and that way."

"I will plant apple seeds all around."

Johnny walked and walked.
He wore old clothes.

He slept under the stars.

And he planted apple seeds.

The seeds grew.

Johnny helped the seeds grow into trees.

People liked Johnny. He helped them.
People called him Johnny Appleseed.

"The apple trees grew up.
Now apple trees are all around."

"What a good story!"